Books designed with giving in mind

Vegetable Cookbook
Kid's Arts and Crafts
Bread Baking
The Crockery Pot Cookbook
Kid's Garden Book
Classic Greek Cooking
The Compleat American
   Housewife 1776
Low Carbohydrate Cookbook
The World in One Meal
Kid's Cookbook
Italian
First Brandy Cookbook
Cheese Guide and Cookbook
Miller's German
Quiche and Souffle
To My Daughter, With Love
Natural Foods

Chinese Vegetarian
Four Seasons Party Book
Jewish Gourmet
Working Couples
Mexican
Paris... and then some
Sunday Breakfast
Fisherman's Wharf Cookbook
Charcoal
Ice Cream Cookbook
Hippo Hamburger
Blender Cookbook
The Wok, a Chinese Cookbook
Christmas
Cast Iron Cookbook
Japanese Country
Fondue

from Nitty Gritty Productions

To young artists everywhere,
especially those at Martin School,
for their help, enthusiasm, and
creativity.

Pat and Rosemary

The Kids Arts and Crafts Book

Written by Patricia Petrich and Rosemary Dalton
Spot illustrations by Patricia Petrich
Full page art by Young Artists

A Nitty Gritty Book*
Published by
Nitty Gritty Productions
P.O. Box 5457
Concord, California 94524

*Nitty Gritty Books -- Trademark
Owned by Nitty Gritty Productions
Concord, California

ISBN 0-911954-33-3

Contents

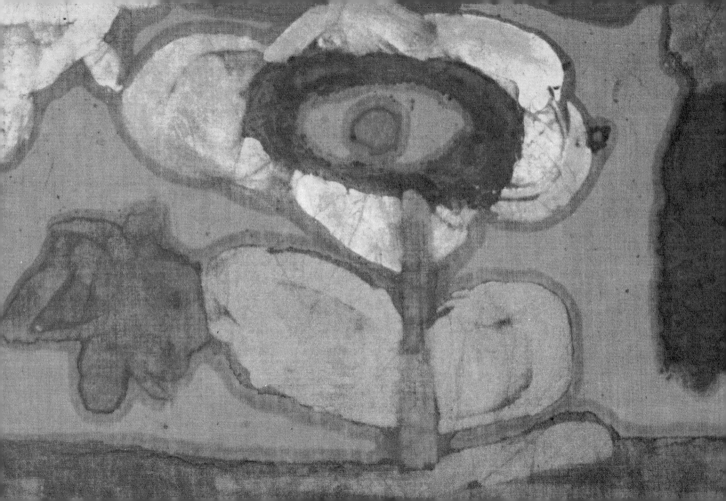

Hi Artists and Artists-to-be,

We hope you like this arts and crafts book and will enjoy the adventure of working with all kinds of art materials and trying all kinds of things.

Think of this book as a starting point for you, a collection of ideas. Use your imagination and ingenuity! You can change any activity and come up with your own ideas and ways of doing things. That's when it's really exciting!

Remember, anyone can be an artist. There is no one way to do anything in art. There are as many ways of drawing, painting, and being creative as there are people.

1

Sometimes you will like the things you do better than other times.

Don't worry when you don't like the way something turns out. Just let yourself go! If you enjoy yourself and are happy with some of the things you create, that's what really matters!

Arts and Crafts Rules

1. Get an okay from Mom or Dad before you start working on a messy art project. Pick a good time too. No one wants a paint-covered wreck at the dinner table, or greeting company at the door.

2. Work in an area where no one minds if you make a mess. Be good to rugs and furniture! Work far away from them.

3. Wear old clothes — something your art project won't ruin — something that's ruined already! Dad's old shirts are good cover-ups.

3

Arts and Crafts Rules (cont.)

4. Put newspapers under your work area, and clean up your tools and your mess when you finish. Sponges, old rags, and paper towels are good clean-up materials.

5. Try not to be too discouraged if something doesn't turn out the way you want it to. Everyone who tries to create has this same struggle sometimes. When you are disappointed in something, walk away for a while. Later things may not look as bad as you thought.

6. Enjoy your finished artwork by putting it on a colored paper or fabric backing, or by framing it, and putting it on display. (Get help and permission from the people you live with for this). Small magnets to hold artwork to a refrigerator door are one good way of putting things up. A scrapbook is a good place to put your artwork too!

7. Things you make can be good gifts for other people - You're giving a real expression of you!

Arts and Crafts Terms

Here are some definitions you may need....

Abstract Art A kind of art that emphasizes lines, shapes and colors.

Blocking In Lightly drawing the main parts of a drawing with circles or squares, then filling in details later.

Collage A picture or design made by gluing an assortment of things together.

Crayon Batik Painting with crayons and dye.

Arts and Crafts Terms (cont.)

Crayon-Chalk Transfer  Making positive/negative pictures by putting chalk and crayon layers on paper and drawing on top on clean paper.

Crayon Resist  Drawing with crayon and painting over it. Crayon wax resists paint.

Crayon Rubbing  Putting paper over textured surface, then rubbing it with crayon.

Diluted Paint Paint thinned by mixing it with water.

Arts and Crafts Terms (cont.)

Mobile — A hanging sculpture or construction.

Mosaic — A picture or design made by gluing bits of paper, tiles, beans, rice, pebbles or other materials.

Origami — The Japanese art of paper folding.

Papier-Mâché — Layers of paper and paste which become strong and hard when dry.

Art Tools and Materials

Here are some things you can use in your artwork. You can think of others too. Add the items you think of to this list.

Of course, you can do a lot of artwork with just a few of these things. And it's surprising what you can create from things that are often thrown away!

Crayons
Tempera or poster paints
Watercolors
Acrylic paints
Colored chalk
Colored pencils
Marking pens
Block printing ink
Brayer
Paint brushes

Construction paper
Newspapers
Magazines
Paper bags
Wrapping paper
Old wallpaper - sample books
Wax paper
Old greeting cards
Egg cartons
Paper plates
Butcher paper
Milk cartons
Cigar, shoe boxes
Fabric scraps

Art Tools and Materials (cont.)

Plastics:

Plastic squeeze bottles

Styrofoam packing materials

Drinking straws

Plastic meat lids

Styrofoam meat trays

Other materials:

Paste, white glue, rubber cement, scissors stapler, tape, erasers

Food:

Spaghetti, macaroni, lasagna, noodles

Beans, rice, corn kernels, dried peas

Washed eggshells (crushed), food coloring

Natural Materials:

feathers	sand	
cotton	leaves	
shells	seeds	
rocks	seed pods	driftwood,
pebbles	nuts	other wood
popcorn	twigs	scraps

Art Tools and Materials (cont.)

Other Materials:

Wire
Buttons
Yarn, rick-rack,
 braid, trims
Corks
Spools
Cardboard tubes
Empty cans
Fabric, felt scraps
Popsicle sticks
Tongue depressors

Toothpicks
Fishing line
Beads
Stamps
Pipe cleaners
Exposed slide film
Ice cream spoons
Hammer, nails
Cupcake papers
Tissue paper
Clay

Hint: Disposable T.V. trays, muffin tins, styrofoam trays and egg cartons are handy things to save for mixing paints.

Art Topics

Everybody has times when they feel creative, but can't think of a thing to draw. Try abstract art- you really don't have to draw a "thing" - or use this list of topics to stimulate your imagination. You may want to add some of your own ideas to this topic list too, so that you have them when you need them.

Bicycle riders
A witche's house
Magic gardens
Dragon
Castle

Balloon ride
Baseball game
Man-in-the-Moon
Motorcycle jump
Hairy-scary monsters

Angel
Snakes
Dinosaurs
Circus
Jungle

Pumpkin house
Cavemen
Airplanes
Submarines
North Pole

Art Topics (cont.)

Christmas tree
Race car driver

Disneyland
Easter Bunny
Santa Claus
Wild animals
Football
Pets
Ghosts
Sailing ships
Trains
My family
Carnival
Robot

Giants
Flowers
Snail
Owl
Space
Seahorse
Spiders
Ballerina

Clown
Robber
Parrot
Butterfly
Pirate
Trees
Throne
Magician

Me, when I'm mad
Something cold or hot
Something glad
And anything else you can think of....

Elements of Design ᴡᴠᴠ

You can use these in all your artwork....

Sometimes when you can't think what to draw, it helps to know the seven elements of design:

◎ ○ ⌒ • ∿∿∿ ᴠᴠᴠ —

You can put these together in thousands of ways, using any art materials you have. ◎◎ ⌒⌒⌒ ☀ ✛ ∿∿∿ ✳

graph paper ↑

Try out some design combinations on newspaper or graph paper. You can create interesting patterns and textures by repeating some designs.

news-paper ↵

Crayon Resist

Paint will not stick to the wax on crayons. Draw a picture or design with crayons, coloring very hard. Put newspapers under your drawing and paint quickly over it. Brush the paint on in one direction only. (Don't keep putting on paint because then it will start to stick). The paint will "bead up" on the crayon. The drawing shows through.

17

Crayon Rubbings

paper clips

tagboard rubbing

You need:
Old crayons with papers peeled off

Newsprint or thin paper

Objects to "rub" or

Tagboard or construction paper

Scissors

Glue

Rubbings are easy to make. Find things with texture or a bumpy surface. Put newsprint or light drawing paper on top of what you want to rub. Hold everything still. Use the side of the crayon and color hard. The image will come off on the paper.

You can also cut things to rub out of heavy paper, such as tagboard. Glue tiny scraps on for eyes and other details, or cut part of the tag-board away.

tagboard stencil

glue on

cut out

You can use these stencils to make many rubbings.

← leaf underneath

Crayon Rubbings (cont.)

Coins

String is good for rubbings because you can put it down, rub, change the design of the string, and rub some more. Possibilities for rubbings are endless: old tombstones and plaques (permission may be needed), manhole covers, old keys, hinges, keyhole plates, even old tree stumps. Happy rubbing!

Leaf

String, thread

Metal gear

Raised plastic

Metal

Lace, rick-rack, trims

More Ways to Use Crayons
Do your own thing!

You can do lots of things with broken or peeled crayons!

Twist the crayon for wings, trees, butterflies and other things.

Use the blunt end or point for dots, large circles.

Dots and circles. ←

Rock the crayon back and forth for a squiggly line, crawly things.

 ← Use the side of the crayon to make tunnels, swirls.

Ways to Use Crayons (cont.)

Use the side of your crayon for ribbons, steps, flags— for a different way of drawing.

Flying carpet ride anyone?

Cut notches in the crayons with a scissors for a different effect too.

Use the side of a crayon to outline cutout shapes.

A mosaic of crayon dots. →

Dots can make a picture too.
Invent other ways with crayons!

Crayon Etching
Fun to do on paper plates too!

Put down newspapers. Crayon heavily on background paper or paper plate. Use one color crayon or several **colors**.

You need:

Crayons
Paper
Paintbrush
Black tempera
Liquid detergent
Sharp tool, such as pencil point, unfolded paper clip

Pour some black tempera in a container. Add a few drops of liquid detergent and **stir** mixture. (The detergent makes the paint stick to the crayon.) Paint this mixture **over the crayoned** paper. Let it dry. Then use a sharp tool to scratch a design or picture. Scratch out large and small areas. The crayon will show through.

22

Crayon - Chalk Transfer

Put newspapers on your work surface. Cover your background paper with a heavy layer of colored chalk — blotches or patterns of different colors next to each other. Be sure the whole paper is filled in with chalk. Crayon <u>heavily</u> over the chalk with black crayon. Put a second piece of paper on top of the crayon-chalk paper. Draw a design or picture with pencil, pressing hard. Shade in some areas. You will have 2 drawings - a positive and a negative! Just like magic!

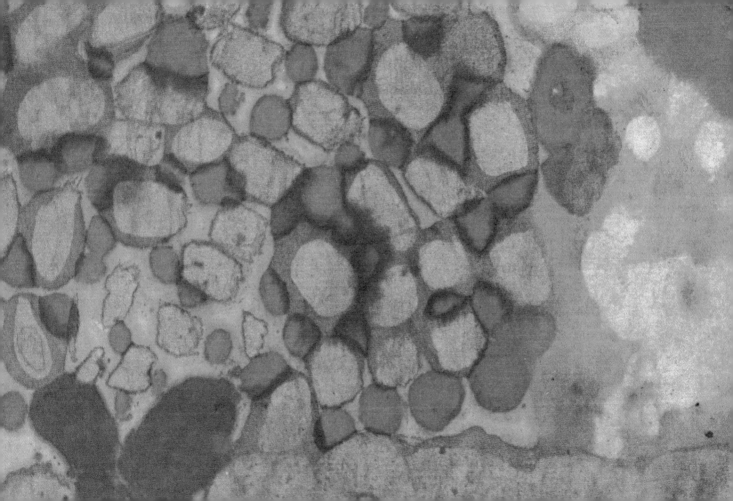

Crayon Batik
A super project! Adult help needed!

You need:
Cut up pieces of
fabric-old sheets,
unbleached muslin,
T-Shirts are great!
Unwrapped crayons
Paraffin cut in ½
inch cubes
Paper towels
Old tempera or water
color brushes
Muffin tin or juice cans
Newspapers
Large pan, iron
1 package of any cold
water dye and
disposable container

Put 3 large unwrapped crayons the same color (or 6 small ones) and 1 cube of paraffin in a muffin cup or juice can. Do this for each color you want.

Be sure an adult is helping! Set the muffin tin or juice cans in a pan of water. Put the pan on a stove or hot plate. Keep

Crayon Batik (cont.)

the heat on low.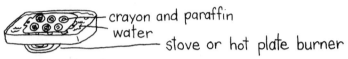

crayon and paraffin
water
stove or hot plate burner

Be sure to keep water in the pan, otherwise wax can be flammable!

Put your fabric on top of newspapers. If you are decorating a T-Shirt, put newspapers inside it, to protect the back. Now, paint with melted crayons. Work fast, leaving some spaces unpainted.

T-Shirts you decorate yourself are great! Brush dye over crayon only, or dye whole shirt.

Crayon Batik (cont.)

Let your crayon wax dry. Then crumble up the fabric to make cracks in the crayon. Shake loose crayon bits into a waste basket, and you are ready to dye your fabric.

Mix dye according to package directions, in a disposable container, such as an empty milk carton. Put the fabric in the dye. Leave it there until you like the color. Take it out (rubber gloves work best)*and lay it on newspaper. Put several layers of paper towel on top and bottom. Iron until wax is gone.

Be sure you still have help, if needed! You now have a batik, and several paper towel batik prints! *Squeeze gently

Paper
towel
T-shirt
Paper Towel and
newspaper

Alphadoodles
Fun on rainy days, too!

You need:
Paper
Paste or glue
Old newspapers
or magazines
Crayons, mark-
ing pens, or
pencils

Pick a piece of white or colored paper for background. Cut out letters, numbers, or words from newspapers or magazines. Or cut some from construction paper. Paste your cut-out on the background paper to make a picture or design. You can add to your picture with crayons, marking pens, or colored pencils.

This is a funny way to make cartoons too. Another project is to make something out of blotches or torn paper scraps. Let yourself go!

Crayon on Sandpaper
Try different kinds of sandpaper....

This is an exciting project because crayons on sandpaper are so colorful! Just crayon right on the sandpaper, pushing hard in some places, light in others. You will have a bright, rough-textured drawing.

You can also make a print from your sandpaper drawing. Place it on a piece of newsprint or drawing paper crayon-side down. Iron the back of the sandpaper with a hot iron. (Get adult help if needed!) Pull the sandpaper and drawing paper apart and you have 2 designs!

Crayon on Crumpled Paper Bag

This project can look like Indian or African art or Hawaiian Tapa cloth, depend-on the designs or drawings you use.

Soak a brown paper lunch bag (or larger bag if you like) in water until it comes a-part. into one piece of paper. Crumple up the bag and squeeze the water out. Open the bag very carefully so it doesn't tear. Let it dry. It will have a rough surface like leather or Tapa cloth— a good background for crayon or paint.

Crayon on Crumpled Paper Bag (cont.)

Decorate the bag with designs or pictures. You can fold creases in it and color designs in the spaces. You can make it look like an African mask, or even an Indian rug or tepee. To make a crayoned bag look more primitive, paint over it with a mixture of half brown paint, half water.

To make a tepee cut a large half circle from your bag (or from a 12 by 18 inch piece of construction paper.) Color a few Indian designs or symbols on your tepee, then overlap the straight edges and glue or staple it to form a cone. Cut a triangle doorway and fold it back. Add a few toothpicks at the top to look like supports.

Drawing

and Painting

Drawing

Pencil outline

Texture drawing

There are many ways of drawing and all kinds of tools to use – pencils, colored pencils, chalks, crayons, marking pens and charcoal are a few.

You can draw from your imagination, or try to draw things as they look to you. (Things look different to each one of us). If you add the lines and patterns of things you are doing "texture drawings". Cartoons are still another type of

Still Life drawing →

(If your dog sits still...)

Drawing (cont.)

Cartoon →

drawing using humor and exaggeration.

    Whatever kind of drawing you are doing, one method that is helpful to know about is called "blocking in". "Blocking in" is lightly drawing the main parts with circles, squares or other shapes, then filling in the details later. When you "block in" a drawing, you get the main ideas down quickly and easily.

    Try to experiment with different ways to draw. The more things you try, the more you can do!

"Blocking in"

Cartooning
Drawing with a sense of humor.

Cartooning is an easy type of drawing to try. Cartoonists make funny lines, faces, and scenes. One way they do this is to exaggerate the things they draw - make them bigger, smaller, simpler or sillier than they really are.

Regular nose

Exaggerated nose

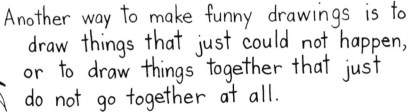

Another way to make funny drawings is to draw things that just could not happen, or to draw things together that just do not go together at all.

To draw cartoons, keep your lines simple, and try to see the funny side

Cartooning (cont.)

of life.

Here are some face shapes and features for you to practice. Put them together to make your own funny drawings.

Ears

Cartoon noses

Beards and mustaches

Face Shapes

Cartooning (cont.)

Eyes

Hair

Mouths

And many more....

Drawing with Words

Think of a word you like. Picture it in your head. Draw a light pencil outline. Then, make the drawing by writing or printing the word over and over again on your pencil outline. You can add to your drawing with tissue, cut or torn paper, or scraps of fabric. (Or, you may want to glue scraps on a background to <u>start</u> your drawing and give yourself ideas). Use the way that feels best for you.

Ways of Painting

Long strokes

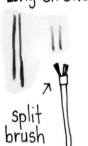

split brush

Twisting the brush

Dry brush

Mixing colors

Color on top of other colors

There are many ways to use your brush to paint. Here are just a few. You can also paint with a square of stiff cardboard, cotton swabs, toothbrushes, pencil erasers, sponges, even old shoe polish bottle-brush containers. Clean and dry your equipment after each use.

Dots (pencil eraser and paint)

Pressing the brush

Dry brush rolled

← Rolling the brush ↓

Tapping the brush

Squeeze Painting

You need:
Empty plastic
squeeze bottles-
mustard, catsup,
detergent bottles
are good.
Paints - Tempera
Liquid starch to
thicken paint
Paper

Put different colored tempera paints in-to empty squeeze bottles. Add a little liquid starch if you want to thicken your paint. Stir well, and put the bottle lid back on.

Squeeze the bottles over your paper to make de-signs or pictures.

For big blobs and thick lines hold your bottle near the paper. Hold the bottle high for thin lines, smaller dots.

Straw Painting

For this project you need construction or rice paper, black tempera paint, straws cut in half, glue or paste.

Thin your paint so it is about half paint, half water. Put your background paper down on newspaper and drop a small blob of paint in the middle. Blow through a straw to move the paint and make a spooky tree, spider, or other idea, such as an Oriental hanging. Let the paint dry. You can cut out Halloween,

Straw Painting

Egg Tree

Christmas, or Easter symbols and glue them on your tree branches, or you can paint them on the branches.

For an Oriental hanging, use dots of paint to make clusters of flowers, or just lay down your brush and pick it up again and again to make another kind of flower cluster. Small twists of tissue or crepe paper could also be glued on to make flowers. Glue dowels at the ends of the paper and hang.

Brush flowers

Christmas Tree

Finger Lickin' Painting
(Tasty Drawings)

You need:

Instant chocolate or butterscotch pudding, or. vanilla pudding with food coloring added.
Shiny paper (shelf paper is good)
Clean hands

Mix the pudding according to package directions. (Get help if necessary). Let the pudding set.

Put down newspapers and wear old clothes. Then you're ready to start.

Put a blob of pudding on the shelf paper.

Use your hands and fingers to make a design or a picture. Finger lickin' good!

Ways to Use Paper

Curl it with a scissors, or by rolling it around a pencil.

Pleat it with folds.

Fold it and make it stand up.

Staple strips to make sculptures.

You can do amazing things with paper. Newspaper is great to experiment with!

Fringe it. Curl it

Cut and fold designs.

fold up or in.

Braid it to make springs and things....

Cut or tear it and glue it to make pictures.

Cut spirals and shapes that hang.

And many other things too....

45

Paper Strip Art

Do things with your paper strips—curl them, bend, twist, cut and fringe them. Glue them on paper over, under, all around each other. It's great to see what you can make paper do!

To curl paper, hold a strip of it against a scissors blade with your thumb on top. Pull and you have paper curls!

> **You need:**
> 1 inch x 12 inch strips of construction paper - lots of colors
> Paste or glue
> 9x12 inch background paper - color you like
> Scissors

Scissors edge

pull

46

Wiggle Snakes
(Accordian Paper Folding)

Hold 2 strips of colored paper like this, one strip in front of the other. Then fold this front strip behind. Next, fold the bottom strip up. Keep folding, one strip on top of the other. When you reach the end, glue your end pieces to keep your snake together. Add a head and decorate.

There are many other ways to use these folded paper strips. Two different colors look better folded than 2 strips the same color. Tapered strips of paper (wide at the top, narrow at the bottom), can be used for a creepier snake or hanging decorations.

Pop!

Pop-Up Books

3 pieces of paper →

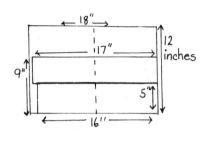

You need: Construction paper, scissors, stapler, crayons or marking pens. This is an easy project!

Cut 3 pieces of paper these sizes: 12 by 18 inches, 9 by 17 inches, 5 by 16 inches. Fold each piece of paper in the middle. Plan a scene or action drawing.

Color a background on the biggest piece of paper. The second biggest piece of paper can have more things

48

Pop-Up Books (cont.)

from the background and some action.
The smallest piece of paper has the rest of the background and action. Cut out the backgrounds of the 2 smallest papers. Staple all 3 papers together at

background

background, action   background, action

both sides. The front and middle picture will stick out. Close your book. Open it and `boing`! - 3-D pictures!

You can make parts of your pop-up book move by having flaps that lift up, and by mounting small pictures on "springs" made Accordian-Folding paper (see p. 47).

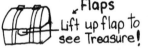

Flaps
Lift up flap to see Treasure!

tape
hinges

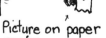

Picture on paper spring.

Slotted Animals

To make animals that will stand up, fold construction paper in half. Cut out the animal's body so it looks like this. On another piece of paper cut out a head, tail, whatever else you want to add. Make a slot on the body near the front and fit in the head. Make a slot at the back and fit in the tail.

Decorate your animal with colored paper, yarn, buttons, wallpaper or fabric – all kinds of scraps.

50

Stand-Up Animals Cars and People too!

Another way to make stand-up animals is to fold construction paper and draw a whole animal under the fold. Use a diagonal fold for animals that are sitting or extra tall.

Cut out and decorate.

Fold paper the long way to cut out people. You can make cars, trucks and other stand-up things too, by folding the paper in half the long or short way. If things won't stand up well, put a staple near the fold.

staple↓

Moving

Torn or Cut Paper Mosaic

Make a pencil drawing. Large pictures or designs work best. Go over your pencil outline with black crayon or marking pen. Use cut paper squares or torn bits of paper to fill in your outline with color. If you are using colored tissue, use white glue mixed $\frac{1}{3}$ part glue to $\frac{2}{3}$ part water. Regular white glue (undiluted) works fine for other papers or fabric. You can add details with crayon or marking pen.

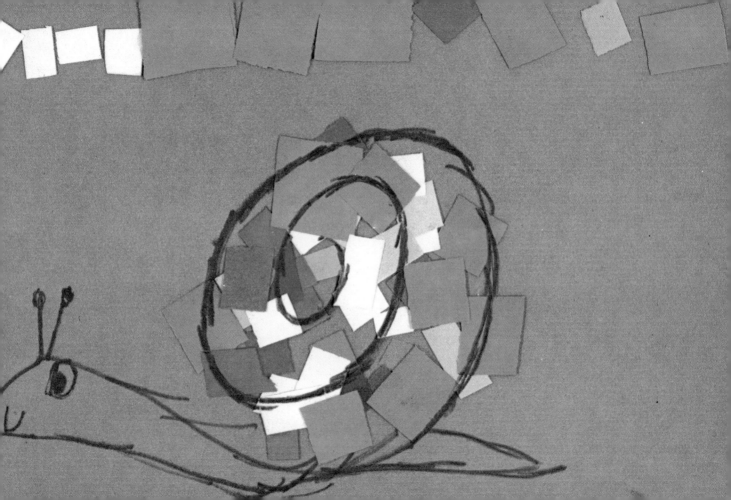

Cone or Cylinder Creatures

You need:
Construction paper
Paper and fabric scraps
Stapler
Glue or paste

You can make all kinds of things - people, animals birds, machines - by starting with a cylinder ▯ ⬭ or a cone △. To make a cylinder, roll the paper and staple or glue it closed. For a cone, cut a half circle ⌣. Then overlap the straight edges and fasten them ◭. Add faces, arms, feet, wheels, yarn or curled paper hair - whatever your creation needs. Happy inventing!

Paper Sculptures

You can make these large or small. Small ones are great mobiles!

You need: Butcher paper, paint, stapler, scissors, newspapers

Draw your animal, creature, or object very large with pencil or light chalk. Cut a front and back the same size and shape. Staple or tape the edges together. Leave an opening big enough to fill the sculpture with crumpled paper, cloth, old nylons, or packing materials.

Now paint your sculpture. Add surface texture with yarn, fabric, feathers, buttons - any scraps you can find. Use your imagination!

Paper Strip Cutting
Cut a series of things...

Fold a strip of paper in half  and
then in half again. Any paper will do—
newspaper too.

Think of what you want to cut. For
scenes that go
across, fold your
paper like this
. Draw or cut your folded paper
so that the picture is attached on
the sides.

Paper Strip Cutting (cont.)

If you want your cutting to be attached up and down, hold your paper like this and cut. Be sure not to cut too much fold or things will fall apart.

fold

fold

whoops!

Origami Frog

You can use regular origami paper for this project, or any paper you happen to have: newspaper, wrapping or tissue paper, or construction paper.

1. Cut your paper into a square ☐. A 5 by 5 square is a good size.

2. Turn your square sideways ◇. Fold in half. ◇---> △fold

3. Fold ends up △ → △ Fold legs down. Fold head down, one fold at a time. Fold edges back. Add eyes, then glue frog on a background or hang it.

58

Merry-Go-Round Mobile

Make a construction paper circle and decorate it. Eight inches is a good size. Cut a slit. ⊙ Overlap the edges. Staple or glue them. △ This makes a cone.

Make Merry-Go-Round figures from construction paper. Color one side, and cut them out. Color the other side too. Attach your figures to the Merry-Go-Round cone with string and scotch tape. Then thread a knotted string ✓ through the cone ⊿ ⟁ knot inside and hang your Merry Mobile!

← knot inside.

←cone

Merry-Go-Round

59

Print Making

Funny Feet
Also called Tenny-Prints
or Sneaker-Prints

ha ha

This is a good project to do in the garage. Step in some DUST (not grease or mud). Then step on a plain piece of paper. You now have a dust-print. Color it however you like.

It's fun to decorate with these! (On the ceiling?) For a great party game make your own outline (or a friend's) and play "Pin on the Feet"). Good cards and bookmarks too!

You need:
Feet-wearing shoes with a design on the bottom. (Check and see...) Crayons, paint or marking pens

Paper

Fishprints

You need:
Fish from a fish market -uncleaned, uncut. Red snapper, rock fish, are good kinds to use.
Water base block printing ink ▭
Brayer ⬁
Small piece cardboard for rolling out ink.
Newspaper
Paper towels
Tissue or rice paper

Put your fish down on newspaper. Spread the fins the way you want them to look. Squeeze about 2 inches of ink onto the cardboard. Roll the ink with the brayer until it is "tacky" or "sticky". Now you are ready to "ink" your fish. Roll the ink-covered brayer all over the fish. If you get ink on the newspaper, cover the ink-spot with paper towel. Now, lift up your tissue or rice paper and lower it

Fishprints (cont.)

onto the fish. Try to get the fish in the middle. Pat the fish gently, all over. Then lift the paper off carefully and let it dry. Your fishprint will look great framed!

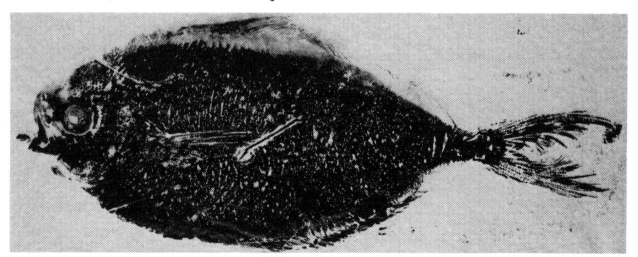

Gadget Printing

Meat mallet

Bobbin

Lids

Fork

Collect gadgets such as forks, spools, bottle caps — things with interesting shapes or textures. Press objects on a printing pad or brush on paint or ink and then print.

To make a printing pad, brush paint or ink on a damp sponge.

Fruits and vegetables print too. So does non-hardening clay with a design cut or pressed in.

Sockets

Spools

Cardboard

Pencil

Fingerprint Art

   This is easy and fun to do.
Just put your fingers on a stamp
pad, then press them on paper.
Add to your print with marking
pens. You can make people, birds,
animals, insects, even a finger-
print circus. Good cartoons! Fun
to use as stationery or frame!

Styrofoam Printing

Wash and dry a styrofoam meat tray. Cut off the edges so that you have a flat piece of styrofoam. Draw a picture or design on the styrofoam with a sharp pencil. Put your tray on newspaper. Roll paint* or water base block printing ink across the styrofoam with a brayer, or brush on ink or paint. Put a piece of paper on top of the inked or painted tray. Rub the paper with your hands, then pull it off carefully. You can make many prints from this tray.

* Tempera paint

Roll-a-Print

Cut a design or picture from light cardboard and glue it on your tube, can or rolling pin. Or, make a design by gluing on string or rick-rack. Let the glue dry overnight. Roll the cylinder across the paint, ink, or stamp pad. Then roll it across your paper to make a print. Great for cards or decorations. You can even make your own party tablecloth!

Box Fun
Milk cartons, egg cartons, large boxes, rolls, tubes....

You can make just about anything from boxes! Construct things large or small. Big box constructions can come to life with you inside! Good places to hide too!

Small boxes can be masks, zoos, doll beds, castles — anything you can invent....

Jimmy, where are you?

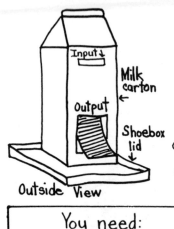

Outside View

Input ↓
Milk carton
Output ←
Shoebox lid ↓

slide ←

Inside View

Feed the Computer
You'll love this project!

Carefully open the top of an empty quart or half gallon milk carton. Wash it and let it dry. Cover it with adhesive - backed paper or glue on construction paper. If you pick solid color paper you can use marking pens to make your milk carton look like a computer or a robot. Other things you can add to make it look real are buttons, paper digits and dials, springs, nuts, bolts, and old Christmas tree lights.

Cut a narrow slit (about 1 by 3

You need:
1 empty milk carton
Adhesive backed paper or construction paper
3 by 12 inch strip light cardboard
Scissors or mat knife (get help
with the cutting if necessary.)
Shoebox lid if you like, to hold
the Computer and cards.

Feed the Computer (cont.)

bleep
bleep

Giant
Packing-Crate
← Robot

inches ▭) at the top of the milk carton. Cut a larger one (about 3 by 3 inches □) 1-2 inches up from the bottom of the carton. Cut a strip 3 by 12 inches from light cardboard. Staple or tape this strip inside the milk carton at the top back.→ Let the other end come out the bottom slot. Staple the top of the carton closed.

Now make question and answer cards from light cardboard about 2 by 3 inches in size. Write a question on one side and put the answer on the back. Feed the Computer question side up, in the top slot. The answer card will come out the bottom slot. Try to say the answer before the card lands. See if you were right. You can use riddles, number combinations, and even quiz show type questions. Playing "Beat the Computer" is lots of fun!

Shrink Shrink Shrink....
Just like magic!

Draw your own pictures to shrink or trace greeting cards, coloring books, comics or photographs.

Outline your drawing on the plastic with a <u>permanent</u> marking pen. Turn the plastic over. Fill in the outline with permanent colored marking pens. Use wide strokes. Color lightly because shrinking makes

You need:
Permanent (not water base) marking pens)
Liver or meat lids (ask your butcher) or shrink plastic from hobby shops
Scissors
Oven + Adult help if necessary.

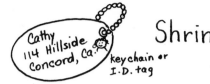

Cathy
114 Hillside
Concord, Ca.

keychain or
I.D. tag

cards
too!

the colors darker than you first made them.

Preheat the oven to 350-400 degrees. (Remember adult help if needed). Cut out your plastic shape. If you want a hole in it use a paper punch. Crumble, then open, a piece of aluminum foil. Put the plastic on top. Put it in the oven or a toaster oven. Watch the plastic carefully. You won't believe your eyes! It will curl, shrink, then unfold and flatten. Take it from the oven with a pot holder and flatten with a book. Great jewelry, key chains, Christmas ornaments, identification tags. Glue on paper to make cards. Super on birthday cakes too!

73

Tissue Paper Flowers
Great in a vase, on packages, hats....

You need:
Tissue paper
Scissors
Pencil
Thin wire
Masking tape
or Florist
tape

Take a sheet of tissue paper 15 inches by 20 inches. Fold in half. Fold again. Then fold in half the other way. Draw a flower petal shape on the folded paper. Cut along your lines (with the paper still folded). Open it and you will have 2 strips with 4 petals.

Refold each strip separately. With a pencil roll each folded strip (to make the petals look real). Start at the top and go as far down as possible. Open each strip carefully and separate the petals. Gather each petal strip around and around a piece of wire.   Strips will go around several times. Wrap the base of the petals and the "flower stem" with tape.

wire →
tape→

Christmas Mobile

← Coat hanger

Mobiles

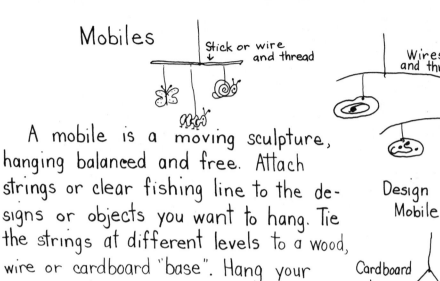

Stick or wire and thread

Wires and thread

A mobile is a moving sculpture, hanging balanced and free. Attach strings or clear fishing line to the designs or objects you want to hang. Tie the strings at different levels to a wood, wire or cardboard "base". Hang your mobile so it can hang freely.

Design Mobile

twigs or sticks

Auto-Mobile

Nature Mobile
Shells, moss, driftwood, etc.

Old umbrella ←

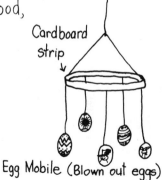

Cardboard strip ↓

Egg Mobile (Blown out eggs)

Collage
Getting it all together....

You need:

Lots of good junk! All kinds of scraps - rough, smooth, soft, shiny. Here are some: Fabric , lace, yarn, rickrack, nuts, bolts, buttons, egg cartons, wood scraps, packing materials, dry cereal, beans, rice, anything else you can think of....

A collage is a picture or design made by gluing all kinds of things to a flat surface. You can use paper, cardboard, burlap- whatever background you like. One way to do collage is to cut out part of a drawing or painting and glue the parts on a background with other shapes and materials.

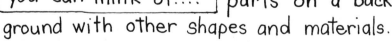

Collage (cont.)

Tissue and marking
pen collage ↑

When you are making a collage, you can put together lots of things or just a few. Pick materials that go with the picture or feeling you are trying to create.

Magazine
picture and
marking
← pen

Pick colors and textures you like together, too. Magazine pictures, photographs and colored tissue paper are interesting to use. Move things around a while before you glue them....

Stamp Art
Stamp collecting is fun too!

You need:
Postage stamps—
from envelopes
or Dime Stores
Glue
Paper
Marking pens, if
you like.

There are many colorful and interesting stamps from all over the world. If you are a collector, save your stamps without cutting. If not, you can make stamp mosaic pictures cutting stamps into small squares or other shapes, and making them into a picture.* Add small details with marking pens, or by cutting small pictures from stamps.

* Don't cut Dad's or Mom's collection!

Pumpkin Man
Make bats or other creatures this way too!

To make a pumpkin man you need light cardboard, brad fasteners and string. Cut out a body, arms, legs and a pumpkin head, separately. Poke holes in the arms and shoulders.
Attach arms at the shoulders with brads in the top holes. Tie a string in the bottom holes and leave it hanging. When you pull on the string the arms go up!
Glue on legs and pumpkin head.
Happy Halloween!

brad
tie
brad
tie

BOO!

Square Pumpkin Box

This can be a Square Santa or Square Rabbit too!

You need a 9x12 inch piece of construction paper, and a ruler. Orange paper is great for a square pumpkin! Measure off a $7\frac{1}{2}$ by $7\frac{1}{2}$ inch square on your paper. Then measure boxes $2\frac{1}{2}$ inches each. Measure an additional box on the center strip. Make this box $3\frac{1}{2}$ inches long, so there will be a 1-inch tab to tuck in. Cut on the dotted lines. Crease lines and fold into a box. Glue or staple the sides.

$2\frac{1}{2}$"

$2\frac{1}{2}$" } Box lid
1 inch tab to tuck in.

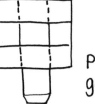

Decorate your little orange pumpkin and fill it with goodies!

82

Ghost Pop-Ups

You need:

Large marsh-mallows

Tissue

String

Someone to scare!

Put a large marshmallow in the center of a tissue. Fold down the tissue and tie a light-colored string below the marsh-mallow. Leave a long piece of string attached. Hook the string over a door or something high. When someone goes by, pull the string and up comes the ghost! If you like, give your ghost marking pen eyes.

Pine Cone Turkeys

You need:
Pine cone or thistle
Pipe cleaners
Colored feathers (Paper or real ones)— Colored feather dusters are good for this, but get permission!

Cut a short piece of colored pipe cleaner for a beak. < Bend a pipe cleaner into a loop for a head, curving the rest of it for a neck. ℓ Twist on the beak, and fit the end of the pipe cleaner into the pine cone.

Bend a long pipe cleaner around the pine cone (between the petals) and bend up the bottoms for feet. Ω Add feathers and your turkey is ready!

Paper curls →

Cylinder Christmas Tree

You need a paper tube or cylinder. Slit one end. Paint the cylinder or cover it with colored paper. Cut a paper Christmas tree and decorate it. Fit the tree into the cylinder so it will stand up.

cut slits ↑

There are many ways to decorate your tree. You can add ornaments of fabric, foil, sequins, buttons, rickrack or other scraps. Or texture your tree by adding paper curls, or cutting slits, half circles or other shapes and bending them.

Holiday Cards

Simple folded shape

Happy ... fold ... fold ... Hanukkah

It's fun to make cards for the holidays you celebrate. Some cards can be simple folded shapes. Others can be cut out.

To make the cut out cards shown, fold your paper in fourths. Refold it in half, and draw your design or symbol on the last fourth. fourth. Cut out the design like this.

fold — cut out

fold

Star of David   **tree**

Refold the card so the design is on the front. Decorate it inside and out with scraps, trims, crayons or pens.

Merry Christmas

fold ... fold

86

Holiday Table Decoration
This makes a good gift.

You need:
Felt shape - get a precut 12 inch square, or cut a shape you like - oval, circle, rectangle
Braid or trim
Miniature ornaments
Glitter, hairspray
White glue

braid
ornaments
← felt
glitter

Pick a color felt and braid or trims you like. Draw a chalk line on your felt where you want to put the braid. About 1 inch from the edge is good. (Use a ruler). Glue the braid down. Put a glue line next to the braid and glue on the tiny ornaments one by one. Spray the area next to the ornaments with hair spray and sprinkle on the glitter. (Hair spray will hold the glitter on but won't show). Leave the center bare so you can put down a plant or some holiday goodies.

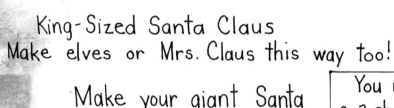

King-Sized Santa Claus
Make elves or Mrs. Claus this way too!

Make your giant Santa Claus any colors you like, or give him a traditional red and white suit.

Cut Santa's face from a 9x12 piece of construction paper. Add a beard of cotton or torn paper. (Paper towels work great). Glue on eyes, nose, mustache. Add a hat. If you want a body, glue Santa's head to a 9x12 inch paper. Cut another 9x12 piece in half for arms and legs.

You need:
2-3 sheets of 9x12 construction paper *
Crayons or marking pens
Glue or paste
Cotton or paper towels
* Santa can be made from scraps of fabric, tissue, wrapping paper, even wallpaper!

And More Ornaments!

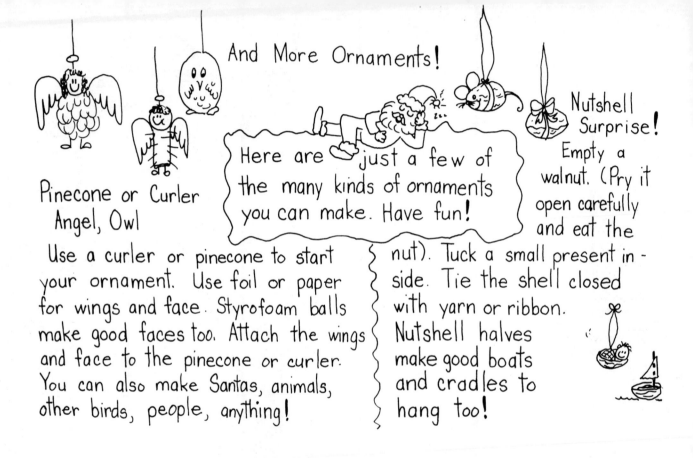

Here are just a few of the many kinds of ornaments you can make. Have fun!

Pinecone or Curler Angel, Owl

Use a curler or pinecone to start your ornament. Use foil or paper for wings and face. Styrofoam balls make good faces too. Attach the wings and face to the pinecone or curler. You can also make Santas, animals, other birds, people, anything!

Nutshell Surprise!

Empty a walnut. (Pry it open carefully and eat the nut). Tuck a small present inside. Tie the shell closed with yarn or ribbon. Nutshell halves make good boats and cradles to hang too!

And More Ornaments! (cont.)

Noodles 'n Glue

Glue noodles of all kinds together. Let them dry on wax paper. Then hang. Good chains too!

Yarn Balls

Cut circles from cardboard. Glue yarn on both sides. (Use bright colors and mix them). Hang from loops of yarn.

Peanut Babies

Draw a face on a peanut. Wrap it in a piece of material. Add hat or yarn hair, and hang.

Hanging Felt Cutouts

Cut out felt shapes. Decorate them by gluing on yarn, sequins, ribbons, or other colors of felt.

Clothespin Dolls or Toys
Good Christmas Ornaments too!

Draw or paint faces on your clothespins. Draw on hair or add string, yarn or cotton. If you want arms, cut them from heavy paper and glue them on.

For clothing find small scraps of fabric and braid. Cut them so they will wrap around the clothespin 1-1½ times. Glue to fasten. Another way to make clothes is to cut the fabric like this ☐ or ☐ and tie it with yarn or string. Add a loop to hang these on your Christmas tree.

You need:
Old fashioned wooden clothespins (Can be found in many hobby shops, hardware stores).
Glue
Marking pens or paint
Scraps of fabric, braid, trims.

Magic Paintings
Great holiday cards too!

Pick a crayon and a piece of paper
the <u>same</u> color. Fold your paper if
you are making a card.
⬜ ▯ or ⬜. Draw
a picture using 1
crayon. (Red cray-
on on red paper,
green crayon on green paper, etc.).
Press hard with your crayon. Add small
details with other crayons if you like.
Now paint over your drawing with white
tempera, and watch how your picture stands out!

Papier-Mâché Ornaments

Crumble up newspaper into the shape you want. Use masking tape to hold the shape. Add ears, feet, and other features of cardboard and tape them to the newspaper. Attach a twine loop for a hanger. Cover the figure with 1-2 layers of newspaper strips. (Dip them in paste, squeeze off the extra, and put them on the newspaper shape). Put on 1 layer of paper towel strips for a final coat. Let your creature dry, then paint it with tempera paint. Shellac it when dry, to protect the paint. (Get help with this part)!

You need:
Wheat paste (mix according to package directions).
Newspaper
Masking tape
Paint, paper towels

← loop
← crumbled newspaper and tape
← cardboard

Christmas Turtle
(Or other animal or creature)

You need:
Old Christmas cards or other cards, or construction paper
Crayon or marking pens
Scissors, stapler

Draw a circle on a Christmas card, other greeting card, or a square piece of construction paper. Cut out the circle and cut 4 slits. Overlap the edges of the slits and staple them (or tape from underneath) to make the shell or body.

 4 short slits

stapled body or shell.

Draw legs, head, tail on construction paper or on pieces of greet-ing cards. Glue or tape the cutout pieces to the shell or body, and bend them until they look real.

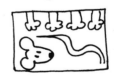

← layouts ↱

Hanukkah or Christmas Mobiles
Crepe Paper Art too!

Cut out symbols for the holiday you celebrate. Decorate them if you like with bits of colored paper, tissue, foil, fabric or other scraps. Hang them on strings from a wire or coat hanger.

Crepe Paper Pictures

You can make colorful holiday pictures using crepe or tissue paper. Cut the paper into quarter-size circles. Twist the circles around a pencil to shape them. Draw a large outline (holiday idea or symbol) on construction paper. Glue on the paper twists of different colors.

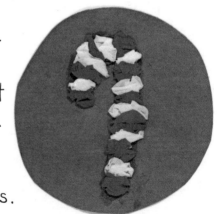

96

Heart Art

Cut out hearts in different sizes, colors. Use all kinds of paper too- construction paper, tissue, newspaper, wallpaper, etc. Fringe the edges of some. Put hearts together to make all kinds of things- spaceships, animals, people, flowers, scenes, designs and Valentines. The heart outlines can be used too. Use crayons, marking pens, and scraps of things if you like.

Love Bug Puppet Valentines

Decorate a small paper bag with crayons, marking pens, paint, and glued on scraps to turn it into a Love Bug Puppet. • Pipe cleaners or folded paper strips (p. 47) make good antennae. Use brown bags or colored ones — pink, white, green or yellow. Make sure to have the bag flap in front so your Love Bug can move its head, and talk.

If you want, write a secret Valentine message under the bag flap!

Secret Valentine message here!

Be Mine!

Gotcha!

Easter Bunny Workshop
(or Easter-Land)

You need 2 pieces of construction paper, one 9 by 12 inches, one 12 by 18 inches. This makes a 3-Dimensional stand-up drawing.

Make your background on the 12 by 18 inch paper. Use crayons, paints, marking pens, or glue on construction paper.

Draw a figure or decorations on the smaller paper. Cut out the paper around the figure, leaving a frame. Tape or staple the **sides** of the front paper to the back page and you have a 3-D drawing.

How to Decorate Easter Eggs

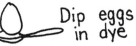 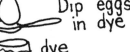 Dip eggs in dye

dye

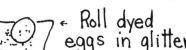 ← Blown out egg

← Roll dyed eggs in glitter

Here are some ways to decorate Easter eggs. Use crayons, pens, egg dyes, glitter, paper, fabric scraps and trims. Egg dyes are available in egg decorating kits. Hard boil eggs or blow them out. To blow out eggs, make a pinhole in each end. Put a dish under the egg and blow in one hole. Decorate the eggshell.

Crayon on eggs. Dip in dye.

  dye

For speckled eggs, add 1 tablespoon of cooking oil to each cup of dye. For lots of colored speckles, dip in different dyes.

Bunnies in the Grass

Hard boil an egg. (Get help if necessary). Draw a rabbit face on the egg, or make it look like a whole rabbit. Use crayon, paint or marking pen. Add fabric or paper scraps for ears, tail and other features.

Glue your bunny rabbit on a small circle of cardboard. Glue on some Easter grass. You can have a whole family of bunnies!

Some other ways to decorate eggs are to make them look like clowns, animals, cowboys, even your friends!

Weave an Easter Basket

You need:
Strawberry or toma-
to basket *
Yarn, strips of
  cloth, or paper,
  leaves or weeds —
  whatever you like.
*Use a laundry bas-
ket for a giant size
Easter basket!

Weave yarn, cloth or paper strips, or natural materials in and out the squares of your basket. Weave around the basket, or stop at the end of each row. If you stop at the ends of rows you can leave pieces hanging out for a nice effect. Use pipe cleaners or a paper strip for a handle. It's fun to surprise someone with an Easter basket!

Photographic Adventure
You can do anything!

Think of an adventure you would like to have. Ask someone to take your picture while you act out your idea (or use a photograph you already have).

Glue your photograph on background paper, and draw or color the rest of your adventure. Or you can glue your photograph to a magazine picture, or a poster.

You are the star or hero of this project. Use your imagination!

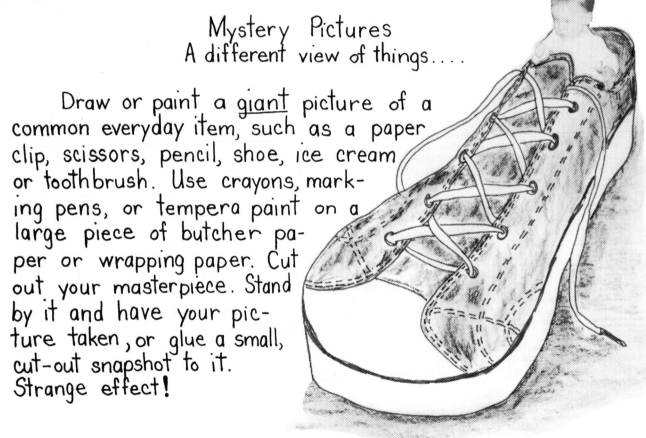

Mystery Pictures
A different view of things....

Draw or paint a <u>giant</u> picture of a common everyday item, such as a paper clip, scissors, pencil, shoe, ice cream or toothbrush. Use crayons, marking pens, or tempera paint on a large piece of butcher paper or wrapping paper. Cut out your masterpiece. Stand by it and have your picture taken, or glue a small, cut-out snapshot to it. Strange effect!

Art on Slides
Adult help may be needed.

You can use old 35 mm slides for this project. Ask an adult to remove the photograph on the slide with a cotton swab and household bleach. The area turns blue first, but with more rubbing it will become clear.

Draw on your clear slide with colored marking pens, ink, or acrylic paint. You can see your picture clearly by holding it to the light, or putting it in a slide viewer. Your slide drawing may be printed into a photograph at your camera store. Keep a collection of your slides and have your own show!

You need:
Blank 35mm slides to write on (Available from a camera store).
Or old (exposed) 35 mm slides, bleach and adult help.
Marking pens, ink, or acrylic paint
Small slide viewer

Art About Me

Collage Self Portrait

You can make a collage that looks like you using practically anything - Scraps of your old clothes, fabric remnants, buttons, trims, etc. Try to pick colors you like, and things that remind you of yourself.

Another way to make your own portrait is to use colored tissue paper. Cut or tear it, and glue it with a mixture of $\frac{1}{3}$ white glue and $\frac{2}{3}$ water. When the tissue paper is dry, you can use marking pens or crayons to add other details if you like.

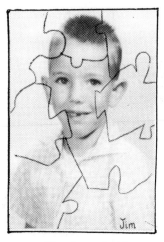

Jim

Your Own Puzzle
Photo Dolls too!

It's easy to make a puzzle of yourself! Glue a photograph (one you can cut up*) to light cardboard. Let it dry, then cut it into a jigsaw puzzle. See if you can get yourself together again! Keep the pieces in an envelope.

Photo Dolls

Photo dolls are fun too! Find a photograph of yourself from head to toe! Get permission to use it, then glue it on light cardboard. Cut* around the cardboard and photo, leaving a stand. You can make up stories about yourself, even make "doll clothes" to wear. Make photo dolls of your family, pets, friends!   * Get help if needed.

Sherry

fold↑   ↑fold

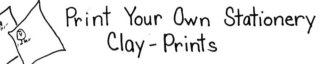

Print Your Own Stationery
Clay - Prints

You need:
Non-hardening clay (plasticine)
Paper
Tempera paint or water base printing ink
Brush or stamp pad (p. 64 tells how to make a stamp pad.)

Roll up a ball of clay the size you want the print to be on the stationery. Pound one side on a table or desk to make a flat surface. Make a design or picture on the clay by drawing on it or pushing into it with a nail, pencil, or similar tool. Now you are ready to print!

Brush the clay with ink or paint or press it on a printing pad. Then press it down where you want your design to be. This method is good for cards, stationery, wrapping paper, and prints to hang.

Name Designs

You need:
Crayons
Paper

Fold your paper in half. Write or print your name on the folded line. Use black or other dark crayon. Press hard. Sherry

Then close the paper and rub the back with your fingernail. This makes the crayon come off on the other side.

rub rub

Like magic! Go over all the lines so they show up.

Decorate your crayon design with crayons, paints or marking pens. It will look great!

Make Yourself a Twin !

You need:
Large paper — butcher paper, newspaper are good.
Crayons, chalks, paint or marking pens
Pencil
Friend

Lay down on a large piece of paper and be as still as you can. Have a friend trace around you with a pencil or light-colored chalk. Use paints, crayons, colored chalks or marking pen to make the drawing look just like you. (If you use colored chalk, spray it with hairspray to keep it from rubbing off.) These giant pictures are fun to put up.
Make a sculpture by tracing 2 outlines.
Wad up newspapers, staple outlines together, and "stuff" yourself!

Silhouettes

Tape a black piece of paper to a wall. (Be sure it's o.k.!) Have your friend sit sideways in a chair near the paper. Turn on a light and the profile will show on the paper. Have your friend sit <u>very</u> still.... (This part is hard!) Trace around the profile on the black paper with a pencil. Cut it out and glue it on white construction paper.

Now it's your turn. Don't wiggle!

You need:
Black and white construction paper (12 inch by 18 inch size)
Gooseneck lamp, lamp with shade off, or filmstrip projector
Pencil, tape

Origami House
It's fun to make this look like your house!

Fold a 9 by 12 inch piece of construction paper in half. Hold it so that the fold is on top. Crease it to mark the center of the house by folding it in half and pinching in a crease. Now fold both ends inward to the center. Fold down the ends to make a roof. This is the outside of your house. Decorate it however you like with a roof, doors, windows, plants, pets and toys. Open your doors and decorate the inside rooms too! Add your family and friends and favorite things.

Hand Puppets

Trace a pattern using your own hand so that it looks like this . (Make it a little bigger than your hand). Cut 2 pieces the same size from paper or fabric. Make sure they are big enough for your hand to fit inside.

Staple or sew the 2 pieces together. Decorate your puppet and have your own puppet show!

117

Finger Puppets

Finger puppet pattern →

There are several ways to make finger puppets. One way is to trace the finger puppet pattern and draw a face you like. Cut it out and adjust it to your finger. Tape the ends so it will stay on. Add hats, ears, jewelry, hair, beards – whatever you wish.

Another way to make finger puppets is to cut the fingers off gloves. (Get permission!!) Then decorate them however you like. Or you can trace a pattern around your fingers, and cut out a fabric puppet. Cut 2 sides for each puppet. Sew together and decorate!

Glove fingers or fabric

chop
snip

Glove

String Puppets

Popsicle stick, wood, or stiff cardboard →

Draw a figure on cardboard in separate pieces. Cut the pieces out. Punch holes as shown. Join the parts with small loops of thread, and decorate.

○ head	▮▮ arms	Puppet layout ↵
▯ body	▮▮ legs →	⊏▭ ▭⊐ ▭

Attach long strings to the head, hands, and feet. Tie the other ends of your strings to a tongue depressor, popsicle stick, or stiff piece of cardboard.

If you find pulling your puppet strings confusing, you can use different color strings.

Cardboard Puppet Theater
An instant stage!

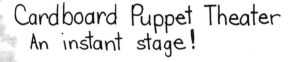

Railroad board or sturdy cardboard is good for this puppet stage. Cut 2 circles about 4 inches in diameter. (Get help if needed.) The holes are for your arms. Put on your puppets then fit them through the holes. Your show is ready to begin!

You can make different "sets" for each part of your puppet show!

Stand or sit to give your performance. Sitting is fun because no one can see you! Make lots of puppets to use with your "stage"!

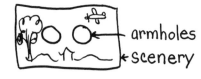

armholes
scenery

120

Magnetic Puppet Show
Great project to do with a friend!

Draw and color puppet figures on construction paper or light cardboard. Make insects, animals, birds, people, storybook characters— whatever you like.

Cut out your puppets and glue a paper clip on each one. If your "stage" is cardboard, glue the paper clip on the puppet back. If you have a shoebox "stage", fold up the bottom of each puppet $\frac{1}{2}$ inch and glue the paper clip underneath

← Paper clip under folded edge.

fold

Magnetic Puppet Show (cont.)

Plan your puppet story. Decorate the shoebox or the cardboard with the background you want. If you are using a cardboard "stage" you can draw different backgrounds on paper, and use paper clips to hold each background on the cardboard as you need it. This way you can change "sets."

If your stage is a shoebox, measure it and cut or fold a paper background to fit inside. Decorate the background and fit it in the back of the box. Now surprise and amaze your friends! Hold magnets behind the cardboard or under the shoebox, and your puppets will move wherever you want them to. Do sound effects too!

Sock Puppets

First get an odd sock — one that doesn't match. Pull it on over your hand so that the heel is over your thumb.

Now add buttons, bows, yarn, all kinds of scraps. Happy Riddle or Puppet Show!

Monster Masks

To make Monster masks, cut out cardboard or corrugated paper. Wallpaper scraps are good too. Add the ugly details and paint.

Hang your mask on the wall, or cut eyeholes, add string, and wear the scariest one of all!

African and Indian masks are great to make too!

Masks

Basic shape.

Staple open-
ing closed,
cut eyeholes

You can **make** many kinds of
masks from manilla paper, light cardboard,
or even paper plates. Start with a basic
shape with a notch in it. Staple it
closed, and add whiskers, mustache,
hair, ears- whatever your char-
acter needs. Keep the mask on
with string.

Guess Who Face
Grocery Bag Masks

You need:
Large grocery
bag- double
thickness
Paint
Good junk-
feathers,
scraps of
things

Put on the bag. (Be sure to get a great big one)! Have someone outside the bag feel and mark where your eyes are. Take off the bag and cut eye-holes. Paint your bag and glue on scraps of things you like.

Yarn is good for hair.
You can be anything!

Box Costumes

Get a box large enough to climb into. Cut a hole you can fit through. Cut 4 smaller holes, 2 in front and 2 in back of large hole. Make straps of cloth or string and stick them through the holes. Tie them to sticks inside the box so that they won't pull out.

Make your box into whatever you like – car, alligator, piano, leopard, bird, train, elephant.... This is great for parties, and for Halloween!

128

Face-Card Costume

You can be anything in this costume – King, Queen, Elf, Cowboy, Batman, Frankenstein, even the Easter Bunny!

Take an 18 by 24 inch piece of construction paper. Cut out an oval shape ⬚ for your face to fit through. Now, draw ears, beards, hats – whatever you want on the new you!

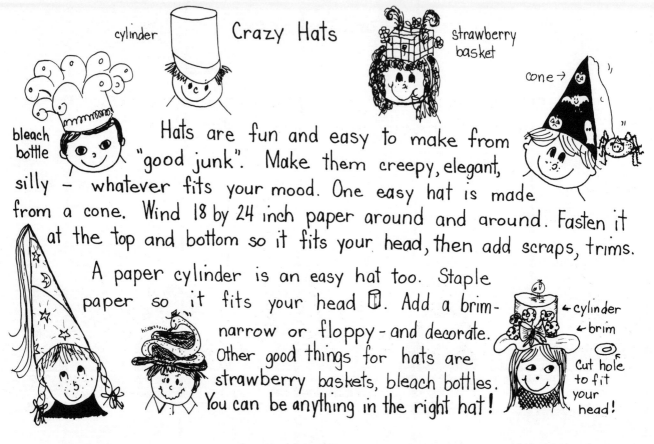

cylinder

Crazy Hats

strawberry basket

cone →

bleach bottle

Hats are fun and easy to make from "good junk". Make them creepy, elegant, silly – whatever fits your mood. One easy hat is made from a cone. Wind 18 by 24 inch paper around and around. Fasten it at the top and bottom so it fits your head, then add scraps, trims.

A paper cylinder is an easy hat too. Staple paper so it fits your head ▯. Add a brim- narrow or floppy - and decorate. Other good things for hats are strawberry baskets, bleach bottles. You can be anything in the right hat !

← cylinder
← brim

Cut hole to fit your head!

hissssssss

A Giant in Disguise
No one will know it's you!

You need:

1 broom
Large paper bag
Newspapers
Old coat
Paint, glue, yarn, weeds
Rubber bands
Baggy pants
Silly shoes

Put a paper bag over a broom. Stuff the bag with crumpled newspapers and tie with string. Paint the bag and glue on hair, nose, anything else you want. Put the coat over the broom and the bag.

Wind rubber bands around the bottom of the coat sleeves. Stuff the sleeves and shoulders with newspapers. Put on baggy pants and someone else's giant shoes. Crawl in and hold onto the broom handle. Peep out between coat buttons, and watch your step!

Spool or Cork Toys

You need corks or empty wooden spools, thumbtacks, paint, paper scraps, and pipe cleaners to make spool or cork animals and other creatures. Paint the spools or corks. Attach the pipe cleaners with tacks. Use paint or paper scraps for faces and added textures or decorations. Feathers, yarn and other scraps may be added too. String spools for great caterpillars too!

← pipe cleaners

tack

Leather - Look Bottle
An instant "antique"....

You need:
Masking tape
Brown shoe
polish
Old rag
Empty bottle

This project is very easy to do. Tear small pieces of masking tape, and completely cover a bottle with them. Overlap the edges. (Some pieces of tape will be on top of others.)

When the bottle is totally covered, rub on some brown shoe polish. Use an old rag to rub the bottle, and wipe off all the extra polish.

Shellac the bottle if you like. (Not necessary- it looks good without shellac too!)
This makes a great gift!

Nutshell Racers

You need:
Walnut half
(Adult help
to get walnut
half)
Glue
Marble
Felt, other
fabric, or
colored
paper

Ask an adult to pry open a walnut shell for you with a sharp tool. (If you are older you can probably do this easily.) Empty the nutshell and glue a marble inside.

Use felt scraps, fabric, or colored paper to add features to your creature — Then find or make a slanted place and have a race. With the marble inside, your creature can really slide! These make good party favors or tree ornaments too!

Go!

Silly Camera
Really a joke!

Watch

the Birdie!

fold 2

Cut a piece of 9x12 construction paper in half. (You only need half.) Fold your 4½ by 6 inch paper like this 📄 and cut 2 slits. (You may need adult help with this part.) Unfold your paper. Cut the slits one more time so they look like this ⊏⋮⊏. Fold the paper again and put the back flap over the front flap.

back flap over front flap

Draw a bird on the flap you fold in front. **Draw a**

Take your picture?

o.k.

136

Silly Camera (cont.)

picture of the person you will "photograph" on the flap under the bird. Make the picture funny if you want. You could even glue a photograph on this flap ahead of time. To "take the picture" pull the paper flaps apart. This will release the picture you drew or glued on. For fun, you can make extra "pictures" to give away (Use small pieces of paper and crayons or marking pens.)

 It's fun to add flashcubes and other equipment to your "camera" too. Just draw or glue on what you want.

Paper Popper
Lots of fun! Easy to make!

Cut a paper 8 inches square. Make 3 creases, just like the picture. Fold the paper in half.

Push the shaded parts in on both sides and you will have a triangle.

Put your first finger between 2 points of the triangle. Snap it! It will open with a pop!

Japanese Carp Kite
Made from newspaper....

You need:
One whole sheet
of newspaper,
ad section
Pencil, scissors,
 glue
Crayons, marking
pens or paint
String
Masking tape

Fold the newspaper in
half lengthwise and draw a fish. Cut the
fish out, but do not cut on the fold. Open the fish.
Make gills, scales and other designs with
crayons, marking pens, or paint.

The fish's mouth must be strong because the
string attaches here. To strengthen the mouth edge,
fold the mouth back about $\frac{1}{4}$ inch twice, and glue or
tape it down. Tape the string around the inside mouth edge.

Fold your fish in half and glue the edges closed. (Not the mouth).
Stuff the fish with small pieces of newspaper, and your Fish Kite is
ready to fly!

139

Spinners
Two Hole Buttons are good spinners too! ◎

Make a circle on stiff cardboard. (Trace around a glass.) Cut it out. Cut out 2 smaller circles and glue one on each side of the large circle to strengthen it. ◎ Now poke 2 holes through the middle of the spinner. (About ¼ inch apart.) Decorate the spinner with crayons or marking pens.

Cut a piece of string about a yard long. Thread it through one hole and back through the other hole. Tie a knot in the string. Put your spinner in the center of the loop and wind up the strings. Alternate spreading your arms apart and bringing them together to keep things spinning!

Copper Foil
Get adult help with this project!

Make several 4 by 4 inch drawings. Choose the best one. (You can use magazine pictures also). Tape your picture onto the copper. (Fold

copper
tape
picture

the tape over the edges) Put your foil on **padding** (newspaper or magazine). Trace over the picture with a ball point pen. Press hard.

You need:
Copper foil- Buy it from a hobby shop- It comes in 4 by 4 inch pieces and many other sizes.
Fine steel wool (oo)
Ball point pen
Copper Sulfate
T-V tray or other disposable item to soak copper in copper sulfate

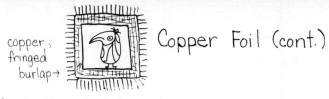

copper,
fringed
burlap →

Copper Foil (cont.)

Take the paper off and re-do all your lines so they are good and deep. Now the foil is ready for the bath!

This part should be done outside or in the garage because copper sulfate has a <u>terrible</u> odor! Mix the copper sulfate in a disposable pan (one you can throw away or use only for this)! Mix it according to directions on the package or bottle. (Be sure to get adult help with this part.) Soak the copper foil in the copper sulfate mixture until it turns black. Put it on newspaper to dry. Then rub the foil with 00 grade steel wool. Leave some places shiny and some dark for contrast. These look terrific mounted on burlap. Pull strings to fringe edges of burlap.

Baker's Clay and Papier-Mâché

Baker's Clay

Pins

Hanging Face Mobile

Hanging Beads, Jewelry

Mix a batch of Baker's Clay, and you can make incredible things - from dinosaurs and other strange beasts to jewelry, toys, sculpture, keychains, ornaments, pendants — even your own zoo!

Get permission to use the kitchen (and ask for help if you need it).

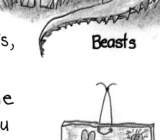
Beasts

Ornaments

Figures

Your own zoo

Plaques

145

Baker's Clay Recipe
Easy to Make!

You need:
Large bowl
1½ cups hot water
1 cup salt
4 cups flour
Aluminum foil

Mix the salt and hot water in a large bowl. Add the flour and mix until sticky. Knead the dough until smooth (about 7-10 minutes). Get help if necessary. If the dough is too crumbly add a few drops of water. If it is too sticky add more flour. Use your clay now, or store it in the refrigerator in a plastic bag until you are ready to use it. Be sure to label the bag so nobody gets a surprise if they nibble!

To bake your clay creations bake in a 300 degree oven for about 1½ hours, turning once. The clay should be hard all through. Leave it in longer if necessary. Get help if you need it.

146

Baker's Clay Methods and Tools
Rolled Out Method

Paint baked and cooled clay with tempera or acrylic paint, or leave it natural. Coat both sides of your clay creations with 2-3 layers of clear nail polish if you want them to last. Let the polish dry between coats. (Or ask an adult to spray both sides with polyurethane -varnish.)

One way to use Baker's Clay is to roll it out with a rolling pin to ½ inch thick. Do this on aluminum foil. Use cookie cutters to cut out shapes you want, or cut your own with a table knife. Bend your shapes or figures the way you want them. To add clay details, roll out the rest of the clay to ⅛ inch thick, cut the details you want, and stick them on your shape with a paintbrush and a <u>little</u> water. You can also "imprint" your clay and give it

147

Baker's Clay Methods (cont.)

texture. Some good tools for this are a bottle cap, fork, pencil, paper clip, toothpick. A garlic press makes great hair or lots of wild squiggles. Stick a hairpin in the top of your object if you need a hook for hanging. Glue a soda pop tab on the back of a larger object to hang it. (Let glue dry 2-3 days.)

Another good project to do with Baker's Clay is your own plaque or sign. Cut a piece of rolled out clay about 5 by 6 inches. Decorate it by imprinting details with tools, or adding bits of clay. Alphabet noodles can be pressed into clay to make your own slogans! Poke holes in your plaque and bake. Paint it if you like. (Coat it with nail polish for protection!) Hang it with twine or yarn.

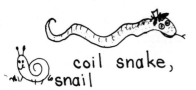

coil snake,
snail

Baker's Clay (cont.)
Pinch Method, Mobiles

Mobiles

Many other things can be made with Baker's Clay by pinching and pulling the dough into different shapes - egg shapes, balls, coils, etc. You can poke holes in these and string them for jewelry or mobiles. Or put them together with a little water to make animals, monsters, people.

You can add yarn, fabric, or other scraps to your creatures after they are baked to give them personality! Mobile faces and figures are fun too. Cut out the parts, poke holes, and bake them. Paint and hang the pieces. Your clay creations are good gifts too!

Pinched and rolled

Papier-Mâché Flower Pot or Bank
(Adult help needed for cutting.)

If you are not a cat lover, do not give up! You can decorate this flower pot however you like. It can also be a bank or funny toy.

First, make a thick mixture of wheat paste,* using package directions. Cut newspaper and paper towel strips about 1 inch wide. Blow up a balloon the size you want your flower pot, bank or toy. Tie a knot in the balloon and cover it with a layer of vaseline. Now you are ready to put on layers of newspaper and paper towel.

Dip strips of paper into the paste. Squeeze off the extra paste. Put a layer of newspaper all around the balloon.

*Or a thick mixture of flour and water.

Papier-Mâché Flower Pot or Bank (cont.)

Then put on a layer of paper towel. Alternate layers. Keep going until you have at least 5 layers. Make the last layer paper towel. Let your balloon shape dry. Then get adult help (if you are making a flower pot) to cut a hole in the papier-mâché. A craft knife is good for this. Pop the balloon and take it out. Make the hole big enough for a flower pot to fit inside. To make a bank instead, just cut a small hole in the top.

Paint your bank, toy or flower pot holder. Pipe cleaners make good whiskers. Attach them with glue. Shellac your finished papier-mâché project if you like. (Get help if needed).

Yarn and Fabric

Design Your Own Fabric

You need:

Permanent marking pens

Muslin or cotton (an old sheet is good).

Newspapers

Put down newspapers before you start. Permanent marking pens can be messy!

You can mark your fabric off in squares or diamond shapes (lightly with pencil) or just draw on it. Squares or diamond shapes are fun because you can draw many different pictures in them.

Some things to make from your fabric are: placemats, tablecloths, pillow covers, wall hangings, quilts, or even clothing if someone will help or do it for you!

153

Ojo de Dios
Eye of God

You need:
2 sticks the same length—twigs, popsicle sticks, round or flat dowels (toothpicks for small ones)
Yarn, twine, thread, string (Bright colors are good.)

Make a cross of your sticks. Wrap the yarn 2 or 3 times around the cross one way, and and 2 or 3 times the other way. Pull the yarn tight.

Now wrap your yarn once around each stick, wrapping in front of each stick, then behind it. Keep doing this, going from stick to stick until the sticks are as full as you want them

Change colors if you like. Start the new color on a

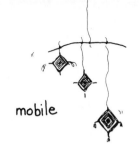
mobile

Ojo de Dios (cont.)

stick, not between sticks.

necklace

These are fun to make with 2 toothpicks or small twigs for Christmas ornaments, necklaces, or mobiles. You can add pompoms ✳ to the ends of the sticks if you like. Or comb pieces of yarn and attach them.

To make pompoms, loop yarn around your thumb and first finger, tie it in the center, and then cut the ends.

making pompoms

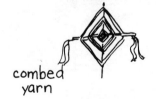
combed yarn

pompoms

Stitchery
Painting with yarn!

You can do all kinds of things with a tapestry needle (one with a big eye ), paper or fabric and some yarn. You can make yarn designs and pictures, or sew scraps of cloth right on fabric or paper. This is called appliqué. Many other things you find

Appliqué

Paper Appliqué

Crayon and Yarn

Stitchery (cont.)

can be sewn on your projects too - shells, buttons, beads, aluminum foil, fur, straws, bottle caps, etc. (If you are going to wear your stitchery, pick materials that are comfortable to wear and easy to wash!)

Hanging With Found Objects

Stitching on Net

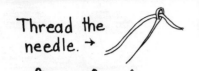

Thread the needle. →

Anchor the needle so it won't fall off.

Stitchery (cont.)

One easy way to start stitching is to make a crayon drawing on paper (or fabric) and outline it with yarn. Cut a piece of yarn about 2 feet long. Thread the needle and "anchor" it by sticking the needle through the short piece of yarn. Pull the needle all the way through the short piece and it is secure — it won't fall off.

Tie a knot in the other end of the yarn and you are ready to stitch. Hold the needle under your drawing. Push the needle point up through the line of your drawing, and pull the yarn

Stitch your favorite drawing.

Stitchery (cont.)

Running Stitch Right-handed

Running Stitch Left-handed

through. This way the knot will be on the wrong side of your stitchery. Here are some stitches you can use to "paint" with your needle.

The running stitch is very easy. Just move the needle and thread in and out of the cloth (or paper), making long or short stitches. If your needle has a big eye, you can thread it with 2 threads of different colors, and stitch 2 rows at once.

Another easy stitch is the cross-stitch. Make a row of slanting stitches and then go back over them

Stitchery (cont.)

Anyone can do it!

in the other direction. You can make stars too. ✳

The backstitch is like a running stitch but has no open spaces. Take a stitch, then go backward to the end of your last stitch. Insert the needle in the same hole where the last stitch ended. Repeat.

Cross-stitch Right-handed

1 ⟨⟨ₒₒₒ⟩   2 ✕✕✕✕

Cross-stitch Left-handed

1 ₒₒₒ   2 ✕✕✕✕

Backstitch Right-handed

Backstitch Left-handed

Stitchery (cont.)

You don't need to know a lot of stitches to do stitchery. Just draw your picture on fabric lightly with a pencil or chalk, pick a stitch or two to try, and have fun experimenting as you go along.

Loose-weave fabrics such as bur-lap or denim are easy to stitch on, and there are endless things you can make, from decorating your own shirt or T-shirt, to making greet-ing cards, Christmas ornaments, Easter eggs, toys, a pillow zoo, or just designs you like.

Weaving

Paper Plate Loom

There are many different ways to weave, and many different materials you can use— yarn, strips of fabric, weeds, twigs, feathers, flat and twisted paper - See what you can discover!

wood

Hanging Stick Loom

Paper Weaving

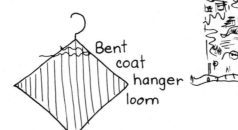

Bent coat hanger loom

A bit of every-thing

Loom made from a wooden frame and nails

Weaving (cont.)

Warp threads

One simple loom is made from a paper plate or an ice cream or coffee lid. Just punch an uneven number of holes in your round object. To make the warp crisscross yarn or thread until all the holes are filled. Then weave over-and-under for a regular pattern, or at random to vary your design.

To weave on paper, cut slits *and weave paper strips or anything pliable between them, such as yarn, weeds, leftover ribbon, straws. These can be used as placemats, wall hangings.... They make good gifts too!

Paper weaving

* Slits can be straight, curved, jagged.

Box
Totem

Nutshell Totem Pole
Other kinds of totems too!

You need a few different kinds of nuts, clay or wood putty, glue, marking pen and paper scraps.

Draw totem faces on the nuts. Join the nuts with clay or putty. Add cut paper wings, beaks and other features with glue or marking pen.

You can also make totem poles by stacking and decorating boxes. Another way is to fold paper to stand up, cut it out and decorate it like a totem.

Cut out

165

Leaf Collages

Collect leaves that have
fallen from trees or plants.
Think of what their shapes suggest.
Use crayons, pens, paints, even photographs or magazine cutouts to turn your
leaves into the wildest things!

N2748 D

Rock Painting and Sculpture

You can do exciting things with rocks! All you need are rocks, imagination, and glue, paint or marking pens.

To make a rock creature or other sculpture, glue your rocks into the shape they suggest, stone by stone. Paint them or leave them natural. You can also paint faces, designs or scenes on rocks, using tempera, acrylic paint, or marking pens.

When the glue or paint is dry, shellac the rock or sculpture if you like. (Get help if necessary.)

Nature Prints

Woodprint and pen

You need leaves, old pieces of wood, or other objects gathered from nature. Put your leaves, wood bits and other scraps on newspaper. Paint them with tempera. Pick up one object at a time, turn it paint side down on paper, and apply firm pressure (for wood) or rub it with your fingers (for leaves). Lift the object off and you have a print. To mix colors, let the first color dry, then print with another color.

Woodprint and pen

Leafprint

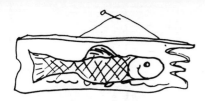

Paint or Crayon on Wood

Crayon or paint can be combined with wood for a nice effect. Collect wood scraps. Think of designs or pictures that would fit with the sizes and shapes you have.

If you decide to use paint, use acrylics or tempera. You can glue on acorns, pebbles, or other natural things that go with your design.

If you use crayon, color heavily on the wood. Place the finished drawing in the oven on low until the colors melt. (Get help if needed!)

Creature Features

teasel and paper

You can make almost anything from things you find on a Nature Walk. Some ideas are wall plaques, mobiles and sculptures.

Combine the things you find. Weeds, teasels or shells look great added to a painting or collage. So do pine cones, acorns, and other found objects. How about a pine cone owl with a seashell beak? Or a painted clown with an acorn nose?

You need:

Driftwood or wood scraps

Things from Nature, such as pine cones, acorns, weeds, seed pods, teasels 🌾, rocks, shells.

Glue, scissors

Construction paper

Wiggle eyes ◎◎, pipe cleaners, if you like

teasel

pine cones

seed pods

Driftwood sculpture

Creature Features (cont.)

Mobile

You can cut apart pine cones to make flowers, an imaginary picture or a design. Arrange the pieces. When you like what you see, glue the pieces together, or on your piece of wood.

I like it!
I'll glue it!

Acorns, pine cones, teasels and shells make good bodies for birds, animals and other creatures. Just add eyes, ears, beaks, tails, legs, wings—whatever features you want for your creature. Some good things to use are shells, pebbles, pipe cleaners, cut paper and pens and wiggle eyes ◉◉ (available from craft stores).

Displaying
Your
Artwork

Displaying Your Artwork

Refrigerator
Gallery

One of the enjoyable things about your artwork is being able to share it with others. You will like looking at some of it when it is finished too!

There are many ways to frame or hang your work to make it look its best. Here are some ideas for you.

The refrigerator can be a great place to display things, using magnets or tape. (Get an okay first). You can hang things on a small clothesline

Harry's Gallery

Displaying Your Artwork (cont.)

Yarn Frame

Fabric Frame

with clothespins too.

It is easy to cut a frame from cardboard in a shape you like- circle, oval, rectangle, square. Change the look of the cardboard frame by the things you put on it. Try to make a frame that goes with what you want to display inside it.

Another idea is to glue on fabric scraps, tucking

Straw Frame

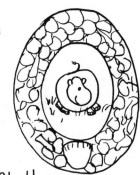

Shell or Nature Finds

Displaying Your Artwork (cont.)

Fringed. Burlap Edges
(Pull strings from edges)

in the edges. Cut up straws can have a nice effect too.

Nature frames can be made by gluing things you have collected onto cardboard, such as shells, acorns or leaves.

For a more simple frame, glue or tape your artwork onto colored paper, fabric or burlap. Fringe the burlap if you like.

Art Fair Today!

175

Introducing Young Artists

Nitty Gritty Productions appreciates the artistic efforts of the following young artists whose artwork appears in this book:

Kevin Attell p. 9, Crayon Resist
Darryll Butterfield p.32, Painting
Ina Canlas Next to Introduction,
 Crayon Batik
Lily Canlas p.76, Collage

Tammy Collins Last Page in Book,
 Painting
Tim Connolly p. 16, String Rubbing
Chris J. Crawford p.132, Alphadoodle
Linda DiSalvo p. 152 Stitchery
Cindy Galea p. 53, Paper Mosaic
Kelly Guilbert p.164, Crayon Resist
Raphael Huerta p. 60, Gadget Print
Sergio Huerta p. 68, Paper Mosaic

Introducing Young Artists (cont.)

Index

Introduction

Crayon Art

Drawing and Painting

Paper Art

Print Making

Junk'n Stuff

Collage

Art About Me

Puppets

Masks and Costumes

Toys and Gifts